MW01659788

The Story of the Grateful Dead

Adrian Hall

LP Longmeadow Press

Copyright © 1993 by Brompton Books Corporation

All rights reserved. No part of this book may be reproduced or utilized in any form or by any means, electronic or mechanical, including photocopying, recording or by any information storage and retrieval system, without permission in writing from the copyright holder.

Longmeadow Press and the colophon are registered trademarks

ISBN: 0-681-20239-4

Printed in Spain

9 8 7 6 5 4 3 2 1

Reprinted and updated 1995

PAGE 1: Ben Friedman's postermat in San Francisco presents a large collection of Grateful Dead posters, album covers, stickers and other assorted memorabilia.

PAGE 4: Bob Weir at the Dead's performance at the Civic Center in Hartford, Connecticut, April 1986.

LEFT: Jerry Garcia wails at the Frost Amphitheatre, Palo Alto, California, May 1989.

The Call of the Weird

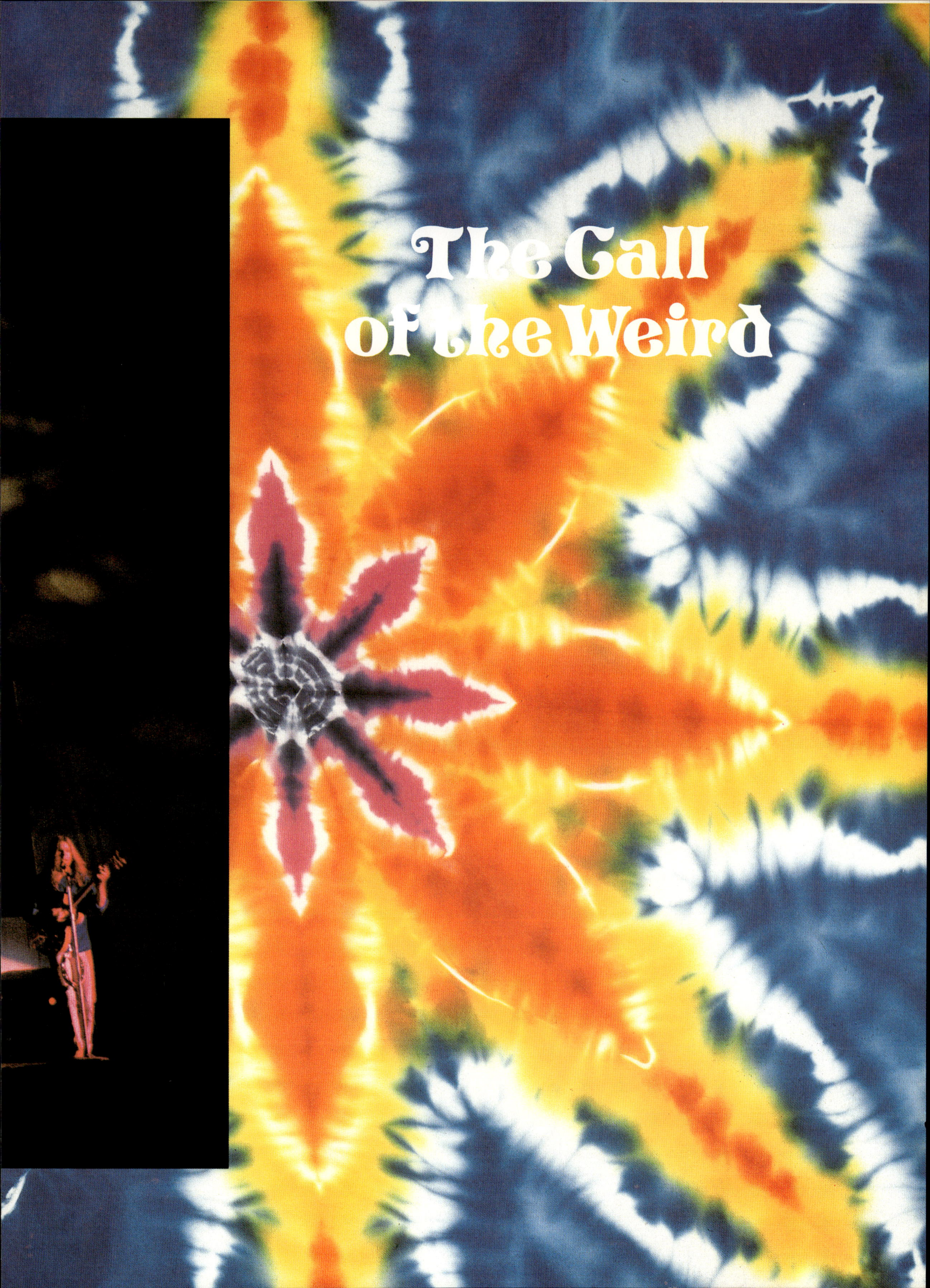

America is a weird place. Throughout the relatively brief history of the United States, strenuous attempts have been made by well-meaning souls to impose a culture that is straitlaced, God-fearing, hard-working, and sober. From the royalists of the 1770s, who thought the Colonies never should have broken away from Great Britain, to the Republicans of the 1990s, who touted "family values," another in their list of code phrases for White, Anglo-Saxon, Protestant morality, America has always been full of right-thinking do-gooders intent on keeping everybody in line. But the line only stays straight for so long, for better or worse.

Maybe that's because, as a mongrel nation founded and settled by outcast religious sects, disinherited second sons, slaves, exiled criminals, refugees from political and economic oppression, and so on, the U.S. never could make the claim that so many homogeneous societies have to being God's chosen people. Maybe, with a cast of characters that large, there was no chance that a single culture or a single set of values could emerge.

PAGES 6-7: The Grateful Dead play the Hollywood Bowl in 1967.

LEFT: The Grateful Dead in the Haight-Ashbury in 1966. Left to right: Phil Lesh, Bill Kreutzmann, Jerry Garcia, Bob Weir, Ron "Pigpen" McKernan.

RIGHT: The Grateful Dead in 1976. Left to right: Mickey Hart, Phil Lesh, Donna Godchaux, Jerry Garcia, Bob Weir, Bill Kreutzmann. Seated: Keith Godchaux.

BELOW: The Grateful Dead, circa 1980. Left to right: Mickey Hart, Phil Lesh, Jerry Garcia, Brent Mydland, Bill Kreutzmann, Bob Weir.

The country overcame remarkably divisive events – the Civil War, the Great Depression – to emerge with an unusual unity of purpose and vision during and just after World War II. But if the war forged temporary agreement on matters of foreign affairs, it also opened a social floodgate, leading to bitter post-war arguments about race relations, political ideals, and cultural values. Should blacks "know their place" or find a new one? Was opposition to Communism justification for persecuting skeptics and dissidents? And what was "good" art and literature and music? What was one to make of a young man like Elvis Presley, who adored his mother, was polite to everyone, and, when he got on a stage, unleashed a violent surge of sexual energy?

Today, Elvis is dead and his image is on a postage stamp, but none of the debates are over. Across America, many people worship God, work hard, and wait for retirement. But then there are others, many others, who, in the word used by the Merry Pranksters, want to go "Furthur" (that's how they spelled it), those who hear what Jerry Garcia once termed "the call of the weird."

And then there's this other thing about America. It's a country of strange obsessives. The screenwriter Steve Tesich (who, appropriately enough, is an immigrant from Yugoslavia) perhaps best described the obsessive nature of U.S. citizens in *Breaking Away*, a 1979 film made by British director Peter Yates. The film concerns four young middle class men living in Bloomington,

ABOVE: Bill Kreutzmann and Mickey Hart, 1990.

BELOW: A grey-haired Jerry Garcia faces the 1990s.

BELOW LEFT: Phil Lesh, 1987.

Indiana, and searching for direction after high school. One of them, for no obvious reason, wants to be an Italian bicycle racer. How he could have conceived such a desire is unclear, but the film traces his disappointments and accomplishments in pursuit of his goal, and does so uncritically. He is, of course, whether or not Tesich realized it, a variation on a Dead Head.

He is also a Trekkie. An Olympic aspirant. A young jazz musician. A Moonie. A bungee-jumper. A chess fanatic. And he is an outlaw. A gold-rush prospector. A hobo. A Hell's Angel. He is a classic American type, a member of any one of thousands of subcultures (many of them, no doubt, subcultures of one) that have existed in the U.S. since it started. Note that we are not talking here merely about people with hobbies. Stamp-collecting is a hobby. Going on a Grateful Dead tour is something else. It's not exactly a vocation, or a career, or a job. Maybe, to use a word that was only invented in the post-WWII era, it's a "lifestyle." Whatever it is, to be a Dead Head is not merely to be a fan of music made by the Grateful Dead.

How the Dead came to inspire the enthusiastic following they have enjoyed for nearly three decades is a long story, only some of which can be told here. And if it has to do with a multicultural national history and a population of "freaks," it also has to do with a particular time and cultural milieu and with a group of individual musicians. And it all started in the back of a music store on New Year's Eve . . . .

BELOW: Bob Weir displays one of his favorite sports of the 1990s.

BELOW RIGHT: Keyboardists Vince Welnick (center) and Bruce Hornsby (right) in 1990.

PASSING
ATORS MAY BE
NTHS, OR BOTH.

The Golden Road, 1964~69

On the evening of December 31, 1963, music teacher Jerry Garcia sat in the back of the closed Dana Morgan Music shop in Palo Alto, playing the banjo, waiting for his students to come for their lessons. The students never turned up, perhaps finding better things to do on a New Year's Eve, but a 16-year-old acquaintance of Garcia's, Bob Weir, did drop by.

"A friend of mine and I were wandering the backstreets of Palo Alto," Weir explained later. "We were way too young to get into any of the hot clubs. We walked by the back door of this music store we used to frequent . . . and we heard banjo music. This seemed strange to us 'cause it was New Year's Eve, so we knocked on the door . . . it was Garcia, who was the local hot banjo player. We knew he had the key to the front of the shop, so we talked him into breaking in, and we grabbed a couple of guitars we'd always wanted to play."

They played for the better part of the night, and somewhere along the way, "we just sat and rapped and decided we had enough talent among us to start a jug band," Weir said. "It got rolling shortly thereafter."

PAGES 12-13: The Warlocks in 1965. Left to right: Jerry Garcia, Bill Kreutzmann, Bob Weir, Phil Lesh, Ron "Pigpen" McKernan.

LEFT: Jerry Garcia in 1966.

ABOVE: Bob Weir in 1969.

ABOVE RIGHT: A contemplative Pigpen in 1969, dressed for once in unusually soft clothing.

RIGHT: Snappy dresser Phil Lesh poses in 1969 in mismatching socks.

If this jam session contained within it the fundamental musical relationship that defined what would eventually be called the Grateful Dead, the other components were already floating around the Palo Alto area, and Garcia knew all of them. He himself had been preparing for a musical career – however circuitously – for most of his 21 years.

Jerry Garcia was born August 1, 1942, in San Francisco. His father, Joe Garcia, was a Spanish immigrant, and his mother, Ruth, was of Irish and Swedish descent, though her family had lived in San Francisco much longer. Joe had been a professional musician, a reed player, but was involved in a dispute with the musicians' union and was forced to seek other employment. He opened a bar and became a bartender. But he named his son after the Broadway composer Jerome Kern.

LEFT: Drivin' that train: The Grateful Dead in one of their first photo sessions, in 1966. Left to right: Bob Weir, Phil Lesh, Pigpen, Bill Kreutzmann, Jerry Garcia.

RIGHT: The Grateful Dead pose at the corner of Haight and Ashbury in San Francisco in 1966. Left to right: Jerry Garcia, Pigpen, Phil Lesh, Bob Weir, Bill Kreutzmann.

PAGE 18: Jerry Garcia poses with a banjo (an instrument he has played on many occasions, though not with the Grateful Dead) at the Dead's residence at 710 Ashbury in 1966.

Jerry Garcia acquired a handicap to being a musician that would have stopped most people: When he was four, his older brother accidentally cut off the middle finger of his right hand below the second knuckle with an axe. Even so, Garcia took piano lessons as a child. His real musical training, however, began when his mother gave him an accordion for his 15th birthday in 1957, which he and his mother took straight down to a pawn shop and traded for a Danelectro electric guitar.

In 1962, Garcia met Bill Kreutzmann when the latter sold him a banjo. Kreutzmann, a Palo Alto native born April 7, 1946, was a teenage high school student and aspiring drummer at the time, and eventually both he and Garcia would be teachers at Dana Morgan Music. They would also play together in a blues band called the Zodiacs that included a teenage blues singer named Ron McKernan whose nickname, given him by Garcia due to his unkempt appearance, was Pigpen.

Pigpen was born September 8, 1945, in San Bruno, California, the son of Phil McKernan, a late-night radio disc jockey who played R&B music. Pigpen grew up loving the blues, singing and playing harmonica, and he first met Garcia at a house called the Chateau in Palo Alto where Garcia lived communally with a group of other musicians.

Though jug band music wouldn't have sounded like his specialty, Garcia asked Pigpen to join in the group he was forming with Weir at the start of 1964. (As a drummer, Kreutzmann did not fit into the jug band format.)

Probably the least accomplished of these musicians, and the least like the others, was Weir, who was two years younger than Pigpen and five years younger than Garcia. Born in San Francisco on October 16, 1947, Weir (whose real name is Robert Hall) grew up in Atherton, an upper class town adjacent to Palo Alto. Weir attended prep school, but suffered from dyslexia and didn't really

find himself until he got his first guitar at 14. He spent his last year at school before dropping out learning to play it, and he also spent a lot of time hanging out in the coffee houses and music stores in Palo Alto, inevitably running into Garcia.

The jug band with Garcia, Pigpen, and Weir was dubbed Mother McCree's Uptown Jug Champions and also included Bob Matthews (later a Dead soundman), Dave Parker (later the Dead's business manager), Tom Stone, and Marshall Leicester, among other people. By the spring of 1965, the trio of Garcia, Pigpen and Weir added Kreutzmann and formed the Warlocks. By summer they had a new bass player named Phil Lesh.

Lesh, born Philip Chapman on March 15, 1940, in Berkeley, was the oldest member of what would come to be called the Grateful Dead, the best educated, and the most musically sophisticated. A classical music fan, he started taking violin lessons in the third grade and was playing the trumpet at 14. He later turned to jazz and to electronic music, studying with such composers as Stockhausen and Berio.

Lesh met Jerry Garcia at the Berkeley radio station KPFA, where he worked as an engineer. When he told Garcia that he was thinking of taking up an electric instrument, he found himself being offered the job of bass player with the Warlocks. He had never played a bass guitar before.

The Warlocks played in San Mateo and Redwood City in August, and began a six-week residency at the In Room in Belmont in September, gradually building up a repertoire and developing a sound. They also played at parties thrown by the novelist Ken Kesey, author of *One Flew Over the Cuckoo's Nest*, at Kesey's home in La Honda. Kesey had become the head of a group of friends who called themselves the Merry Pranksters, and who dropped LSD (legal at this time), which Kesey had discovered when he volunteered for government experiments on

TOP: The Dead's "family," circa 1966. Back row, left to right: Pigpen, Jerry Garcia, Tangerine, Phil Lesh, Rosie, Laird, Bill Kreutzmann. Front row: Danny Rifkin, Rock Scully (the Dead's managers), Bob Weir.

ABOVE: The Grateful Dead on the steps of 710 Ashbury, in 1966.

the drug held in Palo Alto. The Warlocks were no strangers to intoxicants and hallucinogenic drugs – Garcia had first tried marijuana at 15. So, the fit between the group and the Pranksters was perfect.

It merely remained to take the parties public, which occurred for the first time on December 4, 1965 in San Jose, the first "Acid Test." The group would play a series of such events, at which they were only one attraction in a multi-media evening featuring the audience as participants, over the next three months.

The December 4th performance was also the first at which they unveiled a new name: The Grateful Dead. The name refers to a genre of folk tales involving ghosts and charitable acts, and, if somewhat ominous, had an appropriate sound at a time when group names were getting more unusual. Jefferson Airplane had debuted a few months before.

The Grateful Dead appeared with Jefferson Airplane at a benefit for the Mime Troupe, a street-theater group, at the Fillmore Auditorium in San Francisco on Friday, December 10. The event was organized by a member of the troupe, Bill Graham.

Graham, along with Chet Helms (and his organization, "The Family Dog"), were transforming San Francisco into a town where rock music could be heard almost every night. In 1965, the Dead played only a handful of nights in the city of San Francisco; in 1966, they played there 69 times, not counting gigs in the rest of the Bay Area. Many of those gigs were at the Fillmore, booked by Graham, or at the Avalon Ballroom booked by the Family Dog.

The nascent scene was assisted by the poster art of Stanley "Mouse" Miller, Victor Moscoso, Rick Griffin (who would go on to design Dead album covers), and others; the local media; and by record companies. The Dead's first record release was a single pairing the traditional songs "Don't Ease Me In" and "Stealin'," which appeared in June 1966 on the Scorpio label.

The group also was taped in concert, probably in the late summer, at the Avalon Ballroom. Five years later, the tapes were released on two albums by MGM Records' Sunflower subsidiary under the titles *Historic Dead* and *Vintage Dead.* Though not very impressive, the albums provide an interesting look at the Dead's musical direction at the time. They were heavily blues-oriented, with Pigpen very much the band's frontman and lead singer on such tunes as the traditional "i Know You Rider," Sonny Boy Williamson's "Good Morning, Little Schoolgirl," Willie Dixon's "The Same Thing," and a lengthy rendering of the Wilson Pickett hit "In the Midnight Hour," which had come out the previous summer. Other recent covers in the sets included Martha and the Vandellas' 1964 smash "Dancing in the Street" and Bob Dylan's "It's All Over Now, Baby Blue," which had appeared on his

Bringing It All Back Home album released in March 1965. Original material seems to have been at a minimum, though the Dead apparently debuted Garcia's "Cream Puff War" at the Winterland Arena in San Francisco in October.

By that time, the members of the Dead had settled in San Francisco in a house at 710 Ashbury Street in the heart of the Haight-Ashbury neighborhood that had become the center of the San Francisco psychedelic community. Previously, the band had lived in Los Angeles in the spring and, during the summer, at a ranch at Lagunitas in Marin County north of San Francisco. But the house on Ashbury put them in the middle of the scene. And that scene was reaching a kind of critical mass.

By 1967, it would be splashed all over the pages of such national magazines as *Life, Look, The Saturday Evening Post, Time* and *Newsweek*. Even before all that exposure, however, the Bay Area scene had gotten big enough to provoke reaction. On October 2, 1966, LSD became illegal (the Dead played the San Francisco State College "Trips Festival," patterned after a similarly named Acid Test-like event earlier in the year in San Francisco, to mark the occasion), and a month later, arch conservative former movie actor Ronald Reagan was elected governor on the promise that he would stand up to the unruly students at the University of California.

Around the same time, the Dead signed a contract with Warner Bros. Records, a major label based in Los Angeles. They decamped to that city for a few days during January 1967, where, under the watchful eye of producer Dave Hassinger, they recorded an album at RCA Studio A.

LEFT: The Grateful Dead play a free concert on Haight Street, March 3, 1968. Left to right: Phil Lesh, Bill Kreutzmann, Jerry Garcia.

The album, *The Grateful Dead*, released March 17 at the conclusion of a week-long residency by the group at L.A.'s Whisky-A-Go-Go, presents a re-creation of some of the Dead's concert set list, albeit played at accelerated tempos. "Good Morning, Little Schoolgirl," "Beat It On Down the Line" and "Morning Dew" are all still played on occasion by the Dead more than 20 years later.

The album was a moderate seller, getting to Number 73 in the charts. (In the wake of the band's later success, it would go gold – meaning it had accrued $1 million in sales at manufacturer wholesale price – by 1971). More important, though, it gave people outside the Bay Area who had been hearing the odd name "Grateful Dead" a chance to hear what the fuss was about. And it gave the band the opportunity to start playing outside of their usual haunts on the West Coast. They spent the first two weeks of June in New York, appearing at free concerts in local parks and at such clubs as the Cafe au Go-Go and the Cheetah. From there, they eventually would establish themselves around the country.

No sooner had the Dead returned from their first major road trip to New York than they played at the historic Monterey International Pop Festival on June 18, 1967. Though the Dead had agreed to appear, they seem to have seen the show as a sort of L.A. ripoff, and they refused to let their appearance be filmed for the subsequent movie, *Monterey Pop!* They also borrowed the festival's equipment and, in true Grateful Dead fashion, held a free concert at Monterey Peninsula College for the thousands who hadn't been able to get into the festival.

ABOVE: The Grateful Dead at the San Francisco State Trips Festival, the Commons, San Francisco State College, October 2, 1966. Left to right: Bob Weir, Phil Lesh.

RIGHT: The Grateful Dead play at the Great Human Be-In, Polo Field, Golden Gate Park, San Francisco, January 14, 1967.

The summer of 1967 is remembered as the "Summer of Love," the summer when 50,000 or 100,000 (estimates vary) people streamed into the already overcrowded Haight-Ashbury to partake of the peace and love. The Dead, as much as anybody, embodied the hippie philosophy, but they spent that famous summer on the road, playing in the Northwest, Canada, and the Midwest in July and August. They did manage a few Bay Area appearances, notably the funeral of Hell's Angel Chocolate George on August 28 in Golden Gate Park, but these were special shows, not the week-in, week-out gigs of 1966.

In September 1967, the Dead returned to RCA Studio A in Hollywood to begin work on their second album, determined not to rush through it as they had their first. They played a concert at the Hollywood Bowl on September 15 with Jefferson Airplane (now riding high with the hits "Somebody to Love" and "White Rabbit") and Big Brother and the Holding Company under the title, "Bill Graham Presents the San Francisco Scene in Los Angeles," and did a few dates in Denver the following week. By September 29, they were back at the Straight Theater in San Francisco, and there were six of them: A new drummer named Mickey Hart had been added.

Born on September 11, 1943, in New York City, Hart was the son of not one, but *two* drummers, his father, Lenny, being a world champion rudimental drummer, and his mother a former student of Lenny's. Hart himself came into drumming through rudimental and military drumming, which made him a very different kind of player from Bill Kreutzmann, but that didn't prevent him from getting along with the Dead drummer when he

ABOVE: The Grateful Dead at the Hollywood Bowl, September 15, 1967. Left to right: Jerry Garcia, Bill Kreutzmann, Phil Lesh.

ABOVE RIGHT: The Grateful Dead pose for a photo in a barber shop on Haight Street, 1967. Left to right: Phil Lesh, Jerry Garcia, Bill Kreutzmann, Bob Weir, Pigpen.

met him in the mid-1960s. When Kreutzmann took Hart to a Big Brother show at the Matrix, Hart was transfixed. He and Kreutzmann became "drum brothers," as he put it. When he attended the Dead show at the Straight Theater, Kreutzmann invited him up to play the second set. By the time the Dead returned to Los Angeles to resume work on their album, Hart was a full-time member of the band.

Also by that time, Hart was working with a group of musicians, one of whom was out on bail. On October 2, eight narcotics agents, none of whom carried a warrant, arrived at 710 Ashbury and arrested Pigpen, the band's managers, and various friends for possession of drugs. The bust, however, came to nothing and did not slow the Dead's career. If anything, the enormous publicity enhanced their image with their audience.

OVERLEAF, CENTER: The Grateful Dead hold a press conference on October 5, 1967, to complain that their drug bust of October 2nd was police harassment. Left to right: Bill Kreutzmann, Pigpen, Phil Lesh, Rock Scully, Danny Rifkin (managers), Bob Weir, Jerry Garcia, Michael Stepanion (lawyer).

Over the winter of 1967-68, the Dead worked on their album and played shows, sometimes at the same time. In April 1968, they released a one-off single, "Dark Star," backed with "Born Cross-Eyed," which is notable not only as the first appearance of a song that has achieved legendary status with Dead Heads, but also as the first song co-credited to Garcia's old friend Robert Hunter, whose lyrics would have a major impact on the band. (The two songs are available on the 1977 compilation *What a Long Strange Trip It's Been: The Best of the Grateful Dead.*)

The album, *Anthem of the Sun*, was finally released July 18, 1968, a full 15 months after their last album, which, in the 1960s, was an eternity. A trippy album in its time, the LP retains an attraction for Dead Heads, though little of its material is still played by the band and its Number 87 peak in the charts was lower than that of the first album. This was a problem from a business standpoint because, unlike the first album, it was one on which they'd spent six months and a considerable sum of money. After *Anthem of the Sun*, the Dead were in the hole to Warner Bros. for some time.

So, it's no wonder that they were touring continually, though mostly on the West Coast or in the New York area, then and still their strongholds. In August 1968, the Dead played 11 shows, all in California. At two of those dates, at the Shrine Auditorium in Los Angeles, they recorded, hoping to capture their live sound on record (and maybe cut costs). They succeeded, though technical problems with the tapes would hold up release of the result for 24 years, when the terrific *Two From the Vault* album would finally come out.

Meanwhile, the Dead began work on their third album, *Aoxomoxoa*, at Pacific Recording in San Mateo on September 5. Recording continued through January, by which time the band had added a seventh member, Phil Lesh's former roommate Tom Constanten, on keyboards. The touring also continued, with a Midwest swing in November and December as well as the usual frequent West Coast appearances.

By the end of 1968, the Grateful Dead's career was not in the best shape. The San Francisco scene from which they'd emerged had been wracked by publicity, overcrowding, drug epidemics (including a rise in heroin use), and governmental crackdowns; it was moribund. The Dead moved out of the Haight at the end of the year and relocated to Marin County.

Aoxomoxoa, released June 20, 1969, did not change the band's fortunes, but the November 10, 1969, release of the double live album *Live/Dead* was the first representation on record of what a Grateful Dead concert sounded like, from the 23-minute exploration of "Dark Star" that started things off to the gospel coda of "And We Bid You Goodnight." Though the album only reached Number 64, more than 20 years after its release, *Live/Dead* was still Dead Heads' hands-down favorite for the best record the band ever released.

Live/Dead came toward the end of a year that had marked the most extensive touring the Dead had ever done. Crisscrossing the country, they had played 141 shows in California, Illinois, Minnesota, Nebraska, Missouri, Pennsylvania, New York, Nevada, Arizona, Utah, Colorado, Indiana, Massachusetts, Florida, Oregon, Georgia, Washington, Louisiana, and in Canada. They appeared at Woodstock on August 16, though as at Monterey they declined to be filmed or recorded, and they attended, but ultimately did not play at, Altamont on December 6. It was the greatest number of shows they would do in a single year except one: 1970, the most successful year in the Dead's history.

ABOVE RIGHT: **The Grateful Dead at the Newport Pop Festival, Orange County Fairgrounds, Costa Mesa, California, August 4, 1968.**

RIGHT: **The Grateful Dead's lineup from late 1968 to early 1970. Standing, left to right: Tom Constanten, Bob Weir, Bill Kreutzmann, Pigpen, Phil Lesh. Sitting: Jerry Garcia and Mickey Hart.**

A Rare and Different Tune, 1970-79

The Grateful Dead began 1970 at the Fillmore East in New York on January 2 and ended it with their 145th show at Winterland in San Francisco on New Year's Eve. In between, the year contained a number of changes. On January 26, Tom Constanten played his last show with the band. On January 31, the Dead were busted a second time, in New Orleans where they were appearing at the Warehouse. Again, little more than hassles and publicity resulted from the charges.

In February, the Dead began working on their fifth album, at Pacific High Recording in San Francisco. But work had to be squeezed in between their frequent road tours. A hint at the upcoming album's direction was provided on February 8 at the Fillmore West, where the Dead's opening act was the New Riders of the Purple Sage, a country-folk-rock band consisting of the Dead's old Palo Alto pals David Nelson and John Dawson, backed by Garcia on pedal steel, Lesh on bass, and Hart on drums. (The New Riders would continue to open for the Dead during the year, eventually finding full-time replacements for the moonlighting Dead members.)

Even without the New Riders, the Dead were now including acoustic sections in their shows. By February 11, they were back in New York where, on the 13th and 14th, they recorded shows that would turn up on record three and a half years later on the contractual obligation release *History of the Grateful Dead, Vol. 1 (Bear's Choice).* ("Bear" is the nickname of sometime Dead benefactor, LSD manufacturer, and soundman Augustus Owsley Stanley III.) No *Vol. 2* has ever appeared.

PAGES 26-27: The Grateful Dead at KQED Studios, a local television station in San Francisco, August 30, 1970.

ABOVE LEFT: The Grateful Dead at the Olympia Theater, Paris, May 1972. Left to right: Keith Godchaux, Phil Lesh, Jerry Garcia, Donna Godchaux, Bob Weir.

LEFT: Phil Lesh, for one of the few times in his career, sports a full beard, Paris, May 1972.

ABOVE: The Grateful Dead at the Stadium of the University of California at Santa Barbara, May 20, 1973. Left to right: Phil Lesh, Bob Weir, Donna Godchaux, Jerry Garcia.

Workingman's Dead was released in May and proved a watershed for the group. For one thing, the album consisted of eight more or less conventionally structured songs, none longer than 5:42. For another, those songs were presented in a roughly folk-rock style, the lyrics, all penned by Robert Hunter, telling various tales of Americana, with one, "New Speedway Boogie," presenting the Dead's account of what happened at the disastrous Altamont show. It was the most immediately accessible music the Dead had ever made, and it won them a whole new audience. They even scored their first minor hit single, with "Uncle John's Band" (with its "God damn!" exclamation neatly edited out for radio play) going to Number 69 on the charts. The LP itself got to Number 27.

The Dead followed it only seven months later with the similarly styled *American Beauty*, released in November 1970. The album was full of songs that would become permanent favorites: "Truckin'" (which recounts the New Orleans bust), "Box of Rain," "Sugar Magnolia," "Ripple," and more. The album is probably the best-loved studio record the Dead have made.

ABOVE: Jerry Garcia at the Palais des Sports, Paris, September 1974, during the Grateful Dead's second European tour.

LEFT: The Grateful Dead at the Palais des Sports, Paris, September 1974. Left to right: Jerry Garcia, Bill Kreutzmann, Bob Weir, Phil Lesh.

It was also, like its predecessor, a Top 30 hit, and must have helped the Dead's financial posture. But, unfortunately, their monetary status had taken another blow when it came out that Hart's father Lenny, who had been managing the group, had embezzled funds and disappeared. This turned out to be a musical as well as a financial blow when the drummer left the band after a show at the Capitol Theater in Port Chester, New York, on February 18, 1971.

Despite these blows, the early 1970s turned out to be a renaissance for the Grateful Dead. The San Francisco scene from which they came was now long gone, and most of their compatriots had fallen by the wayside: Janis Joplin was dead, and Big Brother was on its last legs; Quicksilver Messenger Service had suffered defections that made it a shadow of its former self; and Jefferson Airplane was scattering into factions from which it would not emerge until years later, under a different name.

But the Dead flourished. In 1971, they played a more sensible 82 shows, during the course of which they recorded material for their second double live album, *Grateful Dead* (often referred to as *Skull and Roses* because of its cover art), released in October. The album introduced more long-time favorites, such as "Bertha," Playing in the Band," and "Wharf Rat," and for the first time contained a message to Dead Heads and an address to write to. Eventually, the Dead's communications with its fans would become the most extensive of any band.

ABOVE: Grateful Dead roadies set up the Wall of Sound prior to a performance at the University of Nevada, Reno, on May 12, 1974.

LEFT: Bob Weir and Phil Lesh onstage in Reno, 1974.

ABOVE RIGHT: Jerry Garcia, Bob Weir, and Phil Lesh at one of the Grateful Dead's few 1975 shows, at Lindley Meadows in Golden Gate Park, on September 28.

RIGHT: The Grateful Dead's rhythm section of the mid-1970s: drummer Bill Kreutzmann and bassist Phil Lesh.

The 1970s was a time when many members of successful groups recorded solo albums, and for once, the Dead went along with an industry trend: Garcia began making his first solo record in July 1971.

In August, Pigpen took a three-month hiatus from the band due to illness. For the next year and a half, until his death on March 8, 1973, Pigpen's presence onstage would be iffy. In September 1971, the Dead began rehearsing with a new keyboard player, and on October 19, at Northrup Auditorium in Minneapolis, Keith Godchaux played his first show as a member of the Grateful Dead. (On New Year's Eve, the band was joined by Godchaux's wife Donna on vocals.)

In January 1972, *Garcia* was released. Though a solo album, it contained a clutch of Garcia-Hunter songs that would be worked into the Dead's live repertoire over the years: "Deal," "Bird Song," "Loser," and others. At the same time, an even more Dead-like solo album was begun, as Bob Weir launched his own solo effort, using the entire band as backup musicians. Released in May, *Ace* also provided songs for the Dead to perform: "Greatest Story Ever Told," "Black-Throated Wind," "One More Saturday Night," and "Cassidy," among others. Taken together, the two solo albums in effect constituted the Dead's follow-up to *American Beauty*.

The material for the Dead's own next album was gathered starting in April when they launched their first European tour, the most extended overseas trip the band ever mounted. It ran through May and resulted in the November release of *Europe '72*, the Dead's only *triple* album, which demonstrated their commercial clout by going gold in only a month.

Europe '72 was the last new material that the Dead delivered to Warner Bros. Records. In August 1973, they began recording their first studio album since *American Beauty*, but rather than signing to a new label, they had determined to start their own record company. This was not just a vanity label, like those several superstar acts now had with the majors. It was an independent manufacturing and distribution company, an unusually ambitious undertaking.

In October, Grateful Dead Records released *Wake of the Flood* by the Grateful Dead, and the album soared into the Top 20. Again, it helped build the Dead's long-term repertoire, containing "Mississippi Half-Step Uptown Toodeloo," "Row Jimmy," "Stella Blue," and "Eyes of the World," songs Dead Heads would learn by heart at the band's concerts from then on.

RIGHT: The Grateful Dead after their return to regular performing in 1976. Left to right: Jerry Garcia, Bill Kreutzmann, Bob Weir, Mickey Hart.

BELOW: The Grateful Dead in 1976, from the vantage point of the keyboard nest. Left to right: Bill Kreutzmann, Keith Godchaux, Jerry Garcia, Phil Lesh, Donna Godchaux.

The album was part of a flood of recordings by the Dead and various offshoots over the next couple of years, albums that kept the Grateful Dead Records pipeline filled. Garcia started a second solo album in January 1974, and the band began working on a new album in March. The solo album, again called *Garcia* (though Dead Heads would refer to it as *Compliments of Garcia*, due to a phrase that appeared on promotional copies), was out in June, an album made up largely of covers such as Chuck Berry's "Let It Rock" and the Rolling Stones' "Let's Spend the Night Together." It had been preceded by the first solo album by Robert Hunter, *Tales of the Great Rum Runners*, and it was followed in a week by the new Dead album *Grateful Dead from the Mars Hotel*, another Top 20 hit containing such songs as "U.S. Blues" and "Scarlet Begonias," though the rapid pace of the band's record-making was starting to show in sometimes second-rate material.

Meanwhile, the Dead had continued to tour extensively, adding to their sound system until they had a massive set of speakers dubbed "the Wall of Sound." But the strain of writing, recording,

touring, and running a record company finally began to tell on them, and in October 1974, they played a final series of shows at Winterland that were filmed and recorded (the last of which featured a returning Mickey Hart) and then called a halt to live work indefinitely.

The Dead's concert retirement did not mean that they had split up. Indeed, they convened again as early as January 1975 to begin work on a new studio album. It didn't even mean that they'd stopped playing live: On March 23, they turned up at Kezar Stadium in San Francisco for a Bill Graham-organized benefit for local schools. And it certainly didn't mean they didn't have new records to release. March saw the appearance of *Old and In the Way*, a bluegrass LP featuring Garcia; *Tiger Rose*, a second solo album by Hunter; and *Keith and Donna*, by Keith and Donna Godchaux. Phil Lesh's album of experimental music with Ned Lagin, *Seastones*, followed in April.

On August 13, the Dead played at the Great American Music Hall to introduce the music from their upcoming album. The concert was broadcast on the radio and in 1991, the Dead finally released it on CD under the title *One From the Vault*. The album it promoted, *Blues for Allah*, appeared on September 1 and

ABOVE: The Grateful Dead in full cry at their favorite venue, Winterland, in 1977, a year they played there nine times. Left to right: Jerry Garcia, Bob Weir, Bill Kreutzmann, Donna Godchaux, Phil Lesh, Mickey Hart.

LEFT: Jerry Garcia at the Civic Auditorium in Stockton, California, on January 18, 1978.

ABOVE: Bob Weir at another of the 1977 Winterland shows.

RIGHT: Donna and Keith Godchaux pose with John Kahn of the Jerry Garcia Band in 1977. The Godchauxs were members of the Jerry Garcia Band in 1977 and 1978.

LEFT: Grateful Dead lyricist Robert Hunter poses in front of the illustration for the Grateful Dead album *Blues for Allah*, November 30, 1977.

RIGHT: Jerry Garcia in Egypt, September 1978.

BELOW: Bill Graham in front of Winterland on New Year's Eve, 1978, prior to a Grateful Dead performance there.

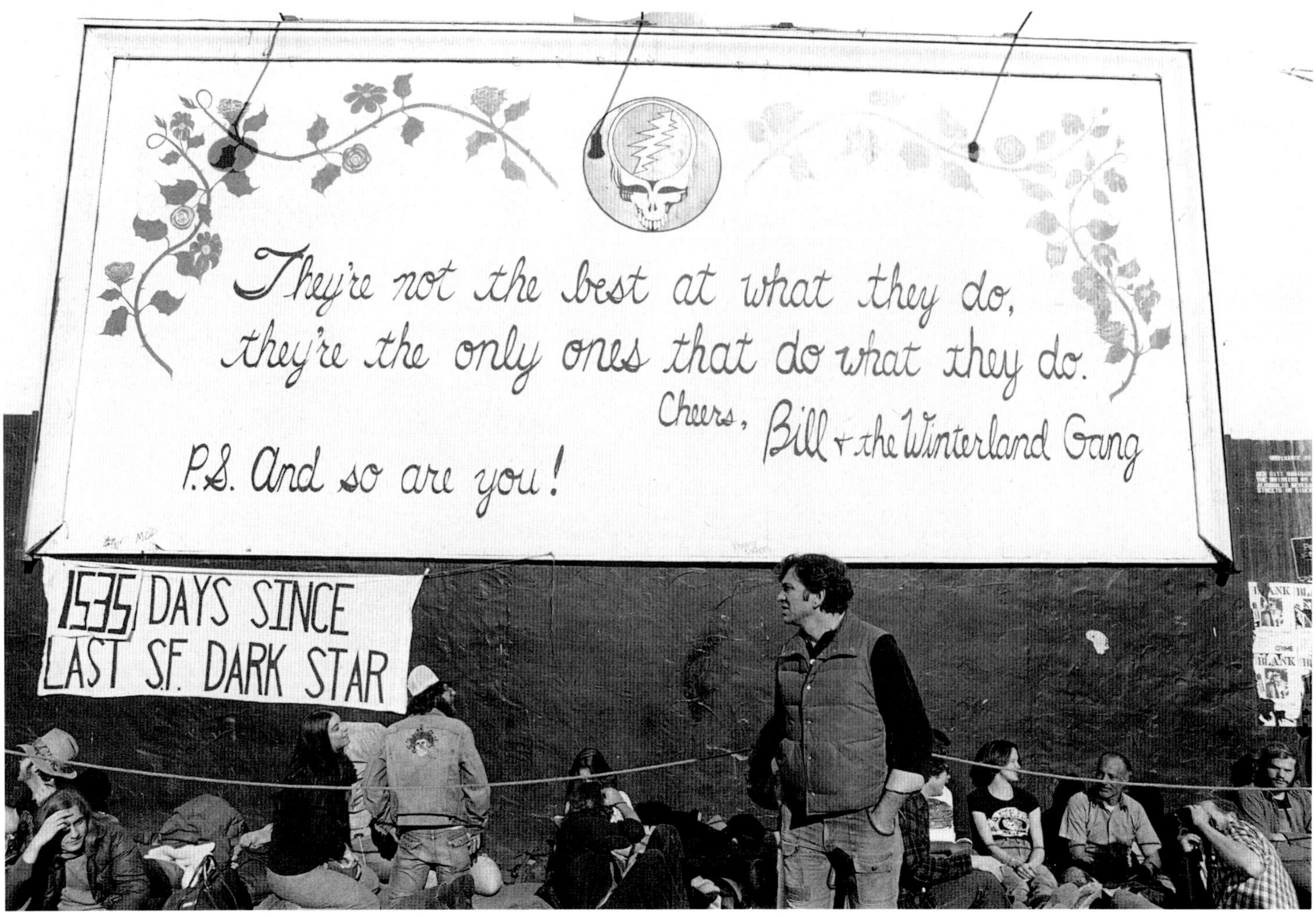

included the "Help on the Way"/"Slipknot!"/"Franklin's Tower" medley that would be played at many shows over the years. The album was the Dead's highest charting so far (and they wouldn't top its peak for another 12 years) at Number 12.

But despite such success, Grateful Dead Records was not able to maintain itself independently, and the next Dead-related releases, Jerry Garcia's *Reflections*, Bob Weir's spin-off group effort *Kingfish*, and Hart's *Diga*, all were distributed by United Artists when they appeared in the first quarter of 1976. When the Dead finally finished and released *Steal Your Face*, the live album from the 1974 Winterland shows, in June 1976, it would be their last album on their own label. (The film based on the 1974 Winterland shows, *The Grateful Dead Movie*, didn't appear until June 1, 1977.)

By the time *Steal Your Face*, perhaps the least-liked album the band ever made, came out, the Dead had come out of retirement and hit the road again. The rest of the year found them touring on a full schedule, after which, as usual, they started a new year by working on a new album.

This time, however, a few things were different. They had signed to a new record label, Arista, and agreed to work with a producer, Keith Olsen, known for his work with Fleetwood Mac. The result was *Terrapin Station*, released July 27, 1977, which contained "Estimated Prophet" and the side-long title song, but did not prove to be a big favorite with the band's fans.

The Dead's concert performances, however, were a different matter. By the time they had returned to touring in 1976, rock tours had come of age, with multi-purpose arenas (primarily used for basketball and hockey) holding 10,000 to 20,000 fans having sprung up around the country. There was, for example, the McNichols Sports Arena in Denver, Colorado, where the Dead played on October 9, 1977, holding 16,500. There was Cobo Arena in Detroit, where they played to an 11,991 capacity on November 1. The Dead also still played theaters where the seats numbered in the four figures, but in such places as the New York area they could play at the racetrack Raceway Park in Englishtown, New Jersey, as they did on September 3, 1977, and still have to broadcast their show live on the radio to satisfy ticketless fans.

Whether they were on the radio or not, the Dead's shows were often – perhaps always – being recorded by Dead Heads by this point as well. Especially after they threw a scare into their fans by retiring, and as the late 1970s saw them releasing increasingly disappointing studio albums, the Dead's live magic came to sustain their appeal not only at their shows but on their fans' tapedecks afterwards. More than perhaps any other band, the Dead were coming to be defined by their fans as much as by themselves.

FAR LEFT: The Grateful Dead perform at Winterland on October 22, 1978, before a slide show from their trip to Egypt the previous month.

LEFT: The Rhythm Devils, Bill Kreutzmann and Mickey Hart, in action in 1978.

OVERLEAF: The Grateful Dead play the closing night of Winterland, New Year's Eve, 1978. Left to right: Bob Weir, Donna Godchaux, Jerry Garcia, Keith Godchaux, Phil Lesh, Bill Kreutzmann.

BASKETBALL
HALL OF FAME

YAMAHA

Nevertheless, they continued to make records – for the moment. Weir's pop-oriented *Heaven Help the Fool* came out in January 1978, and Garcia's fourth studio album, *Cats Under the Stars*, was released in April, though, underpromoted, it was virtually ignored. Many years later, the Dead would revive its lead-off track, the lovely Hunter-Garcia tune "Rubin and Cherise." The Dead began recording their own next studio album in August, this time using Little Feat leader Lowell George as producer. That should have been a good matchup, but the November release of *Shakedown Street* proved it was a misfire.

The band, meanwhile, had scored a considerable coup by gaining permission to play before the pyramids in Egypt, which they did on the evenings of September 14, 15, and 16. Not too many Dead Heads were able to make the trip, and nothing has been released from the shows, but they added to the Dead's legend.

When Dead Heads could hear the band, however, they were becoming less enchanted with the music, largely due to Keith and

BELOW: Keyboard player Brent Mydland at his first Grateful Dead concert, April 22, 1979, Spartan Stadium, San Jose, California.

ABOVE: The Grateful Dead at Red Rocks Amphitheatre in Morrison, Colorado, a venue that became one of their favorites in the 1980s, August 12, 1979. Left to right: Jerry Garcia, Bob Weir, Bill Kreutzmann, Mickey Hart, Phil Lesh.

Donna Godchaux, who fit in less and less well. Finally, the couple was dismissed in early 1979, playing their last date at the Oakland-Alameda County Coliseum on February 17. The Dead then auditioned keyboard players and selected Brent Mydland, who had played with Weir previously. Mydland debuted with the Dead on April 22 at Spartan Stadium in San Jose.

The changeover may have slowed the Dead's recording plans, since they didn't release a new album for a year. In the meantime, new songs began to creep into their sets: "Althea" and "Lost Sailor" were first played on August 4, 1979, at Oakland Auditorium Arena, "Easy to Love You" (written by Mydland with lyrics by Weir's collaborator, John Barlow) turned up August 14, at the McNichols Sports Center, "Saint of Circumstance" was debuted at the Civic Center in Glen Falls, New York on August 31, and a new Hunter-Garcia song, "Alabama Getaway," was unveiled November 4 at the Civic Center in Providence, Rhode Island.

After the start of 1980, the Dead began recording. Back on the road, "Far from Me" was played for the first time on March 30 at the Capitol Theatre in Passaic, New Jersey, and "Feel Like a Stranger" turned up the next night. All of these songs were on *Go to Heaven*, which was released on April 28. As any Dead Head knows, they stayed in the band's set over the next 10 years, but the album has been highly criticized by fans, and is among the Dead's least popular. They would not attempt another new studio recording for seven years.

All Around This World, 1980-85

At the dawn of the 1980s, the Grateful Dead could make the claim to being an odd sort of American institution. They hadn't sold many records in 13 years of making them – when the 1974 Warner Bros. compilation *Skeletons From the Closet* went gold on March 14, 1980, it was only their fifth gold album out of 19 releases – but they had established themselves with a fervent audience who often followed them from city to city on their regular tours (they never played less than 60 shows a year between 1977 and 1985) to see how their unplanned sets would vary and to tape the results for future trading and listening.

Go to Heaven was a more commercially successful album than the other studio albums the Dead had made for Arista. It peaked at Number 23 in the charts and stayed among the 200 best-sellers for 21 weeks, while a single version of "Alabama Getaway" crept as high as Number 68 in the singles chart. But clearly the Dead and Arista had not achieved a broad commercial breakthrough, and as the band approached its "official" 15th anniversary on June 7 (dated by Phil Lesh from when he agreed to join the band) it determined to focus on its strength: live performance.

After extensive touring during the summer, the Dead moved into San Francisco's 2200-seat Warfield Theater for 15 shows starting September 25, during which they returned to their format of including an acoustic set along with two electric ones. They brought back several Dead originals and covers for those sets that fans hadn't heard in years, and they recorded the proceedings. Then, on October 22, they moved to 5874-seat Radio City Music Hall in New York for eight more shows. This stand had its problems – Radio City officials objected to a large skeleton being displayed on the Hall's facade,and they were not enamored with the casual behavior of the Dead Heads – but the Dead were able to record and film there as well.

The result was two new live double albums, *Reckoning* and *Dead Set*, and a concert video, *Dead Ahead*, that was shown on the HBO cable TV channel and eventually released on video cassette. *Reckoning*, taken from the acoustic sets, was released on April Fool's Day, 1981. *Dead Set*, electric music, followed in August as the band completed the summer leg of the annual tour with shows in Tempe, Arizona, and Las Vegas, and prepared to set off for a fall tour of Europe.

Although *Dead Set* turned out to be the last Grateful Dead album released for six years, there doesn't seem to have been any deliberate intention on the band's part to suspend recording. In fact, at least at first, solo projects continued to appear. Weir's new spin-off band, Bobby and the Midnites, a pop-rock-jazz

PAGES 46-47: The Dead play one of their acoustic sets in the autumn of 1980.

ABOVE LEFT: Bob Weir in 1979 at a photo session for the release of *Go to Heaven*, the last Grateful Dead studio album for more than seven years.

LEFT: A photo of Jerry Garcia from the *Go to Heaven* photo session.

ABOVE: The Grateful Dead's publicity photograph to accompany the release of their *Go to Heaven* album, taken in late 1979. Left to right: Jerry Garcia, Bob Weir, Phil Lesh (above), Brent Mydland (below), Bill Kreutzmann, Mickey Hart.

fusion outfit featuring Brent Mydland and former Mahavishnu Orchestra drummer Billy Cobham, released its self-titled debut album in November 1981.

Typically, new material began to creep into the Dead's concerts in 1982, seemingly in preparation for a new album. On August 28, 1982, at the Oregon County Fair in Veneta, Oregon, the Dead premiered two songs: "Keep Your Day Job" and "West L.A. Fadeaway." The first, with a sentiment expressed in its title that was not entirely to Dead Heads' liking, would be one of the group's most controversial numbers in the more than three years it continued to turn up in their shows. Finally, it was abandoned without ever appearing on a Dead album.

TOP: The Grateful Dead's New Year's Eve shows have become legendary for their staging. Here's the 1980 show.

ABOVE: Former Quicksilver guitarist John Cipollina (far left) joins the Dead on New Year's Eve, 1980.

RIGHT: A sea of balloons descends on the New Year's Eve show, 1981.

Much better received was a song introduced at the Capital Centre in Landover, Maryland, on September 15. Although its much-repeated tag line was "I/We will survive," the song was called "Touch of Grey," and it was both the catchiest tune the Dead had produced in a long time and also an appropriate renewed statement of purpose for the veteran band. Two days later came the debut of a politically oriented Bob Weir song, again one with a chorus that did not form its title. "Ashes, ashes, all fall down" was the chorus, but the title, it turned out, was "Throwing Stones."

These songs did not appear on record immediately, but, in November 1982, Jerry Garcia released his fifth solo album, *Run for the Roses*, which featured the touring band Garcia maintained, a band that seemed to play somewhere in the Bay Area practically every night the Dead had off.

New songs continued to turn up in the Dead's sets during their spring 1983 tour. Weir's "My Brother Esau" appeared at the first Dead show of the year, March 25 at Compton Terrace Amphitheatre in Tempe, Arizona. "Maybe You Know," by Brent Mydland, was played for the first time April 13 at Patrick Gym at the University of Vermont in Burlington. Two days later came "Little Star," a Bob Weir song, though it would be dropped after a couple of months. A more long-lived new song was Weir's "Hell in a Bucket," which appeared at the Greek Theatre in Berkeley on May 13.

But though this seemed to constitute enough material for a new album, the months went by without any mention of a recording. Instead, new cover songs began to appear in the sets: the Koko Taylor hit "Wang Dang Doodle," and the Beatles song "Revolution."

The story was not much different in 1984. Brent Mydland introduced "Don't Need Love" at the group's first show of the year, a benefit for their charitable organization, the Rex Foundation, held on home ground at the Marin County Veterans Auditorium on March 28, and on April 23 came a one-time-only performance of Mydland's "Only a Fool" in New Haven, Connecticut. (Neither of these songs would ever turn up on a Dead album.) Just as frequent, however, were the rock 'n' roll oldies. On June 14, the Dead began doing a version of Traffic's "Dear Mr. Fantasy"; on June 27, they played the Beatles' "Why Don't We Do It in the Road" for the first time.

By this point, the idea of a new album, at least as far as Dead Heads were concerned, had come to seem irrelevant. Weir released a second (and last) Bobby and the Midnites album, *Where the Beat Meets the Street*, in August 1984, but as far as the Dead's fans were concerned, their concerts contained an

LEFT: Bob Weir onstage at Frost Amphitheatre, Stanford University, Palo Alto, California, October 1982.

RIGHT: Jerry Garcia onstage at the Greek Theatre, University of California, Berkeley, May 1982.

BELOW: Skulls-and-roses stage adornments at the Greek Theatre, University of California, Berkeley, May 1982.

adequate mix of new and old material, much of it performed differently every night, to keep things going fine. In fact, especially after Dead soundman Dan Healy introduced a "taper's section" behind the soundboard where Dead Heads could openly set up their recording equipment, starting October 27, 1984, at the Berkeley Community Theatre, this period in the Dead's history came to seem a new renaissance, especially in the light of what occurred a few years later.

For a while, the Dead and their songs were the exclusive province of Dead Heads. Since the shows were sold out in advance, the only way to get to see the band was to stay in contact with the Dead office, which sold half the tickets to each show, the other half going to the local promoter. And the only way to hear their latest music was to see a show or obtain a copy of a tape of a show from another Dead Head.

And so the shows continued to evolve. Toward the end of the

LEFT: The Grateful Dead onstage before an elaborate tie-dye-style backdrop, the Greek Theatre, University of California, Berkeley, May 15, 1983.

BELOW: Jerry Garcia and former Quicksilver Messenger Service guitarist John Cipollina, a frequent guest at West Coast shows, trade licks at the Grateful Dead's May 15, 1983, appearance at the Greek Theatre, University of California, Berkeley.

year, the Dead debuted more new and old material: Howlin' Wolf's "I Ain't Superstitious" on Halloween; the Spencer Davis Group's "Gimme Some Lovin'" on November 2; Willie Dixon's "Down in the Bottom" on November 3; the Beatles' "Day Tripper" and Mydland's new "Tons of Steel" on December 28. Of these, only "Tons of Steel" would ever be formally recorded.

It was business as usual in 1985, the year of the Dead's 20th anniversary, 71 shows beginning with a local series in Oakland and Berkeley in February and March, continuing with an East Coast tour in March and April, more local dates in April, a Midwest tour in June and July, a Southwestern sweep in August and September, a Southern tour in October, more East Coast dates in November, and the by-now-traditional New Year's shows in Oakland. Newly introduced songs included Dylan's "Just Like Tom Thumb's Blues" and "The Mighty Quinn," Eric Clapton's "Keep on Growing," the coda of the Beatles' "Hey Jude" tacked onto "Dear Mr. Fantasy," and Wilbert Harrison's "Kansas City."

It seems entirely possible that things might have gone on exactly like this indefinitely, with the Dead being a kind of quasi-1960s jukebox to the delight of their hard-core fans, had not Jerry Garcia taken ill in the summer of 1986.

We Will Survive, 1986–92

Nineteen eighty-six began, as usual, with the so-called "Mardi Gras" shows in Oakland in February. Then came the spring East Coast tour, with the Dead premiering Dylan's "Visions of Johanna" in Hampton, Virginia, on March 19 and Bo Diddley's "Road Runner" two nights later. On March 25 came more Dylan: The lengthy "Desolation Row" turned up in the set at the Spectrum in Philadelphia.

There were extensive West Coast dates, several of them Rex Foundation benefits, in April, May, and June, and then, for once, a change in schedule. Appropriately enough for a band that was playing Dylan music almost every night, the Dead hooked up with Dylan himself, who was touring with Tom Petty and the Heartbreakers during the summer of 1986, for some outdoor and stadium dates. The first came on June 26 at the Hubert H. Humphrey Metrodome in Minneapolis, and the mini-tour continued at Alpine Valley in Wisconsin (a favorite outdoor venue) and River Bend Music Center in Cincinnati, without Dylan and Petty, then a date at the Rubber Bowl in Akron, a Fourth of July show at Rich Stadium in Orchard Park, New York, and two shows at Robert F. Kennedy Stadium in Washington, D.C., with Dylan and Petty.

Then, back in San Francisco, Garcia became ill and fell into a diabetic coma. The guitarist, who was the nearest thing the band had to a leader (and without whom the Dead would be virtually unimaginable) had put on weight in recent years, and, though little firm knowledge was available, fans always feared the ravages of past or present drug use. Diabetes was something they hadn't expected, but the feared result was the same. Garcia was at first given little chance of survival, but he came out of the coma.

He then spent several months recovering, even to the point of having to re-learn to walk and talk, not to mention to play the guitar. Amazingly, he did those things relatively quickly. By October 4, 1986, Garcia was back on stage with the Jerry Garcia Band, and the Dead were able to play their traditional New Year's shows to end a difficult year. But it wasn't the last time Garcia's health would complicate the Dead's future.

The scare seems to have energized the Dead to re-involve themselves with the recording end of the music business. They resumed their usual touring schedule in 1987, recorded a new album for the first time in seven years, and rehearsed with Bob Dylan, this time with the intention of touring as his backup band, not just as co-headliners. Viewers of MTV, the music television channel, were treated to their first Grateful Dead video on June 19 (a night the band spent at the Greek Theatre) when "Touch of Grey" premiered. The single was followed on July 6 (two days after the first Dylan/Dead show at Schaefer Stadium in Foxboro,

Massachusetts) by *In the Dark*, most of whose songs dated from years before.

The result was a surprising explosion of popularity for the Grateful Dead, unlike anything they'd experienced before. Both the single and the album soared into the Top 10, the first time the Dead had reached such sales peaks. Suddenly, a band that had shunned the trappings of mass popularity and the more commercial aspects of the record business was embraced: They had come up from the underground.

For their part, the Dead continued to tour stadiums with Bob Dylan through July, then continued on to their usual haunts, finishing out the summer with dates in the Southwest, then a fall tour on the East Coast that included six nights at the Civic Center in Providence and five at Madison Square Garden in New York, followed by the usual series of late autumn dates on the West Coast leading up to the New Year's shows.

Already, however, something was different. Frequently, now, Dead shows didn't just attract the faithful – those long-haired, tie-dyed Dead Heads who swung and swayed and hoisted their microphone stands – but also a large segment of the standard rock 'n' roll crowd, rowdy refugees from Def Leppard concerts expecting to behave as they usually did, and expecting the Dead

PAGES 56-57: The May 1992 show at Shoreline Ampitheatre, Mountain View, California.

PAGES 58-59: The Grateful Dead onstage at the Frost Amphitheatre, Stanford University, Palo Alto, California, May 1986.

LEFT: The Rhythm Devils in action at the Frost, May 1986.

BELOW LEFT: Brent Mydland onstage with the Grateful Dead at the Frost Amphitheatre, Stanford University, Palo Alto, California, May 1986.

BELOW: Bob Weir and Bill Kreutzmann accompany Bob Dylan during one of the Dylan/ Dead shows, July 1987.

to put on a show to rival the big-time rock acts of the day. Angry letters from Dead Heads began to turn up in fanzines like *Relix* and *The Golden Road*, decrying this trend, and over the next few years, a gradual audience adjustment took place, as some of the new fans departed, and some were converted.

At the same time, the band's new visibility shined a light on the gypsy caravan style of the long-time fans, to their and the band's disadvantage. Communities came to resent the influx of carefree Dead Heads that accompanied an appearance by the band, and law enforcement agents began to crack down on drug use and vendors who sold an extensive array of unlicensed merchandise. In some places, the group was summarily banned from ever performing again.

LEFT: The Jerry Garcia Acoustic Band onstage at the Lunt-Fontanne Theatre, New York City, October 1987. Left to right: Sandy Rothman, John Kahn, David Nelson, Garcia.

BELOW: Bob Weir onstage at Calaveras County Fairgrounds, Angel's Camp, California, August 22, 1987.

RIGHT: Bob Weir sings lead during the Dead's East Coast tour, September 1988.

BELOW RIGHT: Bill Graham, dressed as Father Time, rides to the stage on a mirror ball, New Year's Eve, 1988, Oakland, California.

The Dead themselves tried to deal with these problems. They discouraged vending at almost all locations, wrote letters to their fans about concert behavior, and went on the radio to ask people without tickets not to congregate at their shows. And, by the recessionary days of the late 1980s and early 1990s, communities began to realize that the visiting Dead Heads could mean an influx of money into the local economy. Gradually, things seemed to settle down.

By mid-1988, the Dead had again begun to insert new songs into their sets, introducing Weir's "Victim or the Crime" on June 17 at the Metropolitan Sports Center in Bloomington, Indiana, Garcia's "Foolish Heart" on the 19th at Alpine Valley, and Mydland's "Blow Away" on the 20th. More would follow. This time, fans would not have to wait quite so long to hear the songs on record.

Nineteen eighty-eight was notable also for the Dead's most overt political work since the 1960s, as they announced a major benefit for preserving the rainforests. It was the ninth show in a series they performed at Madison Square Garden in September, and featured Bruce Hornsby and the Range, Mick Taylor, Suzanne Vega, Hall and Oates, Jack Casady, and Olatunji.

On January 31, 1989, the album *Dylan & the Dead*, taken from the July 1987 shows, was released. It did little credit to Dylan or the Dead. The band itself undertook its usual touring throughout the year, though, starting in the fall, they seemed to be cooking up something slightly different. For the October 8-9, 1989, shows in Hampton, Virginia, they were billed as "formerly the Warlocks,"

LEFT: A view of the stage from behind the tapers' section at Cal Expo Amphitheatre, Sacramento, June 9, 1990.

RIGHT: The Grateful Dead onstage at Shoreline Amphitheatre, Mountain View, California, June 1990, one of Brent Mydland's last California shows.

RIGHT: Brent Mydland onstage at Shoreline Amphitheatre, Mountain View, California, on June 15, 1990, the first of three shows there.

and they began to bring back some old material that hadn't been performed in years, notably "Dark Star," last done in 1984. Reportedly, a new live album was in the works.

The next studio album, *Built to Last*, appeared on Halloween. It did not enjoy the success of its predecessor in record stores or with Dead Heads. What did impress Dead Heads, however, was a date on the spring 1990 tour (March 29 at the Nassau Coliseum) when jazz saxophonist Branford Marsalis (previously unfamiliar with Dead music) turned up onstage to jam. The results were recorded and would turn up on the ensuing live album.

But the Dead's momentum was slowed unexpectedly during a tour break on July 26, 1990, when Brent Mydland died of a drug overdose. The death was a shock to the band and to Dead Heads, and the Dead scrambled to find a replacement. When they launched a fall tour on September 7 in Richfield, Ohio, Vince Welnick, an ex-member of the Tubes, was sitting behind the keyboards. He was joined by Bruce Hornsby for selected dates as of September 15 at Madison Square Garden in New York. *Without a Net*, the live album released in September, became Mydland's epitaph.

LEFT: Vince Welnick, former keyboardist for the Tubes and Todd Rundgren, in 1991, the year after he joined the Grateful Dead, replacing Brent Mydland.

RIGHT: Jerry Garcia in the 1990s.

BELOW: Jerry Garcia plays with the Grateful Dead's new keyboard section, part-time member Bruce Hornsby, here playing accordion, and Vince Welnick.

Despite the inevitable musical adjustments necessitated by the addition of one and sometimes two new members, the Dead did not alter their fall 1990 touring plans, which called for their first European dates in nearly a decade. The European tour, which ran for two weeks from mid-October to the first of November, took the band through Sweden, Germany, France, and England. They were followed by a large number of Dead Heads, but at least a few Europeans got to hear what a Grateful Dead concert was like. The Dead returned to play dates in the West and Southwest through the end of the year.

The fall of 1990 was also notable for the first publication of a book written by a member of the Grateful Dead. Drummer Mickey Hart came out with *Drumming at the Edge of Magic* (Harper Collins), in which he traced his own personal biography as well as the details of his lifelong search through the world of percussion. The book sold a healthy 75,000 copies.

Simultaneously, Hart issued a new album, *At the Edge*, which became a substantial success in the new age music market. Hart had pacted with the innovative CD record company Rykodisc, which also issued a series of his recordings of international percussionists and ethnic musicians under the rubric "The

LEFT: Dead Heads flocked to Europe to see the band in October 1990. Here, a fan is glimpsed before the Brandenburg Gate in Berlin.

BELOW LEFT: Vince Welnick onstage with the Grateful Dead. He gradually fit himself into the band's sound in 1990 and 1991.

BELOW: Jerry Garcia onstage at the Zenith, Paris, October 28, 1990.

BELOW RIGHT: Bob Weir onstage at the Zenith, Paris, October 28, 1990.

World." And as if that weren't enough, Hart had undertaken archival efforts on behalf of the Smithsonian Institution, helping to restore the vintage recordings from the catalogue of Folkways Records, which the Smithsonian acquired at the end of the 1980s.

Dead lyricist Robert Hunter, meanwhile, published *A Box of Rain* (Viking Press), a collection of his song lyrics, many of which, of course, had graced Grateful Dead songs. Hunter hit the road to promote the book, accompanied by former Dead keyboardist Tom Constanten. Hunter's performances were recorded for a live album, also called *A Box of Rain*, which was released on Rykodisc in 1991.

Another Dead side project involved Jerry Garcia, who was upping his musical activities. Garcia had recently appeared on a Country Joe McDonald album, *Superstitious Blues*, and kept up

LEFT: Bob Weir at the Shoreline Amphitheatre, Mountain View, California, on August 18, 1991.

RIGHT: Phil Lesh, sporting a six-string bass guitar, at the Shoreline Amphitheatre, Mountain View, California, on August 18, 1991.

BELOW RIGHT: Jerry Garcia at the Bill Graham memorial concert, November 3, 1991, at Polo Field, Golden Gate Park, San Francisco, California.

appearances with his Jerry Garcia Band, but on February 2 and 3, 1991, he also turned up at the Warfield Theater in San Francisco with bluegrass mandolin player David Grisman, who had been a member of the 1970s group Old and In the Way with him. The two played a mixture of material, everything from B.B. King's "The Thrill Is Gone" to Irving Berlin's "Russian Lullaby." The eventual result was an album, *Jerry Garcia/David Grisman*, released on Grisman's Acoustic Disc label later in the year.

But that was far from the end of Garcia's solo activities. He also was enjoying gallery shows of his psychedelic art, in San Francisco, Washington, D.C., and New York. Soon, his work would be turning up on the cover of a Grateful Dead album, among other places.

The Dead itself launched its annual touring for 1991 with the Mardi Gras shows at the Oakland-Alameda County Coliseum on February 19, celebrating the start of another year by breaking out "New Speedway Boogie" for the first time in more than 20 years. The East Coast tour began at the Capitol Center in Landover, Maryland, on March 17, and ran through April 9 at the Arena in Orlando, Florida.

The same month, Grateful Dead Merchandising, the band's mail-order division, which had begun reissuing many of the old Grateful Dead Records releases on CD, put out *One from the Vault*, with Dead soundman Dan Healy announcing that it was only the first of a series of vintage recordings soon to come. Arista Records, the Dead's label for new recordings, meanwhile issued

Deadicated, a tribute album on which Dead songs were interpreted by the likes of Elvis Costello, Los Lobos, Midnight Oil, Bruce Hornsby, and others. Some proceeds from the record were donated to the Rainforest Action Network and Cultural Survival.

The western branch of the 1991 tour commenced on April 27 at the Sam Boyd Silver Bowl in Las Vegas and ran through May 12 at the Shoreline Amphitheatre in Mountain View, California, one of the band's favorite venues, with a final stop at the Coliseum in Los Angeles on June 1. The Dead then headed east again, opening their summer tour on June 6 at Deer Creek Music Center in Noblesville, Indiana, and ending up June 28 at Mile High Stadium in Denver.

As usual, Jerry Garcia had managed to sneak in a few dates with his Jerry Garcia Band here and there, back at the Warfield when the Dead was off the road. He had also found the time to amass a new solo album, on two discs, fittingly titled *Jerry Garcia Band*. It was a live album containing extended versions of such songs as "Dear Prudence" and "Tangled Up in Blue."

BELOW: Jerry Garcia with an acoustic guitar, his instrument of choice on several non-Grateful Dead projects of the 1990s.

RIGHT: The Grateful Dead perform at one of the 1992 Mardi Gras shows.

Bob Weir, meanwhile, also snuck in some dates with renowned bass player Rob Wasserman, the duo sometimes calling their collaboration "Scaring the Children." The two even turned fashion models for the Gap clothing stores, identified as "musicians appearing on behalf of the Rainforest Action Network."

But the busiest Dead member must still have been Mickey Hart, who finished a second book, *Planet Drum*, this one more of an ethnomusicological travelogue in search of ethnic percussion. An accompanying album, also called *Planet Drum*, was released and became a runaway Number 1 hit on the world music charts. Hart gave concerts and lectures to promote the book during the course of the summer. He also turned up on Capitol Hill on August 1, wearing a suit and tie, to talk to the Senate Special Committee on Aging about the healing powers of music for the

elderly, stressing, of course, the healing powers of percussion. Not to be outdone on the literary front, Robert Hunter published his first book of poetry, *Night Cadre.*

In August, the Dead played a series of shows at the Cal Expo Amphitheatre in Sacramento and back at Shoreline, then headed off for their fall tour, which began September 4 at the Coliseum in Richfield, Ohio. It included nine nights at Madison Square Garden in New York and six nights at Boston Garden. The music magazines were reporting that 1991 was a disastrous year for touring musicians, but nobody told the Dead, who, as usual, enjoyed sell-out crowds nearly every night.

During the course of the tour, Garcia was interviewed frequently, his remarks turning up in local newspapers and the national press, and he told more than one reporter that he would like to see the Dead take a six-month hiatus from touring, primarily in order to write new material. (Although it had now been two years since the release of the last studio album, the Dead were not even introducing new songs into their shows, much less planning another record.) But the days were gone (if, indeed, they had ever existed) when Garcia spoke for the entire band, and nothing firm was announced about such a temporary retirement. Dead Heads breathed a sigh of relief that turned out to be premature.

On October 25, 1991, Bill Graham was killed in a helicopter accident. Graham had been closely associated with the Dead and with the San Francisco scene in general for 25 years. When the Dead closed their October 27 concert at Oakland-Alameda County Coliseum with Bob Dylan's "Knockin' on Heaven's Door," there wasn't much doubt who they were singing about.

The formal memorial concert for Graham, however, was held on Halloween at Polo Field in Golden Gate Park. "A Benefit for Laughter, Love, and Music," the show featured a remarkable lineup, befitting the master of concert promotion: the Dirty Dozen Brass Band, Bobby McFerrin, Jackson Browne, Aaron Neville, Tracy Chapman, Santana, Robin Williams, Journey, Crosby, Stills, Nash and Young, the Dead, Joan Baez, and Graham Nash and Kris Kristofferson.

BELOW: Bob Weir was also using an acoustic for solo ventures in the 1990s.

The Dead were joined by harmonica player John Popper of the Dead-influenced band Blues Traveler for a version of "Wang Dang Doodle" and by former Creedence Clearwater Revival leader John Fogerty for a Creedence mini-set featuring "Born on the Bayou," "Green River," "Bad Moon Rising," and "Proud Mary." But the Dead finished their show with an encore of Dylan's "Forever Young" and their own survival anthem, "Touch of Grey." Two months later, they held their usual New Year's shows at Oakland Coliseum, but it wasn't the same without Bill Graham.

The end of the year brought two new Dead-related releases from Grateful Dead Merchandising. One was *Devout Catalyst*, an album by Ken Nordine, a monologuist, whose wild, spacey tales were accompanied by the playing of Jerry Garcia and David Grisman. The other was a new Grateful Dead album, *Infrared Roses*.

Infrared Roses was not a new Dead album in the usual sense, however. Boasting a computer graphics skull image developed by Garcia on its cover, the album consisted of recordings taken from the "Space" and "Drums" interlude parts of Grateful Dead concerts, as electronically treated by Dead technician Bob Bralove.

These musical interludes, long a staple of the second sets at Dead shows, had grown increasingly complicated during the 1980s with the onset of MIDI synthesizer technology that allowed the sounds from ordinary instruments to be altered in virtually unlimited ways. More than just a double drum solo and some jazzy instrumental playing, "Drums"/"Space" had evolved into an elaborate sound landscape in which Bralove and Dan Healy interacted heavily with bandmembers. *Infrared Roses* was the first recorded example of the developments.

Early in 1992, Bob Weir joined the ranks of Dead members who had published books by co-authoring a book and accompanying tape with his sister Wendy called *Panther Dream*. Published by Hyperion Books, *Panther Dream* was a children's book about the rainforest. Weir also turned his environmental attention to adults in March, when the *New York Times*, on its Op/Ed page, published his article, "Forest for Sale: It's a Steal," in which Weir expressed his opposition to the Montana National Forest Management Act, intended to open millions of acres of Montana to industrial development.

The Dead, meanwhile, apparently not heeding Garcia's call for a hiatus, had launched an even heavier than usual tour schedule at Oakland with the Mardi Gras shows on February 22. They had, however, nevertheless found time to write some new songs, and the first show introduced Garcia's "So Many Roads." Far more surprising was a new song sung by Phil Lesh called "Wave to the Wind." On the 23rd, Vince Welnick introduced his first-ever Dead song, "Way to Go Home," while Bob Weir played a brand-new song with an old title, "Corrina." All four songs would recur frequently during the band's 1992 concerts.

Rather than breaking after the Mardi Gras shows, the Dead launched their spring tour within a week, opening on March 1 at the Omni in Atlanta. They then moved on to Hampton, Virginia, the Capitol Center in Landover, Maryland, the Nassau Coliseum in New York, the Spectrum in Philadelphia, Copps Coliseum in Ontario, and the Palace in Auburn Hills, Michigan, where the spring tour ended on March 24.

Grateful Dead Merchandising unveiled its second vintage recording, *Two From the Vault*, in the spring, and the 1968 concert proved a tribute to the musical leadership of Pigpen. The release was exactly what Dead Heads wanted – a great show they didn't already have on tape – and more was promised.

Jerry Garcia couldn't keep his fingers idle for long, and by the end of April he was back at the Warfield with the Jerry Garcia

RIGHT: Members of the Lithuanian basketball team, which won a bronze medal at the 1992 Barcelona Olympics, wearing the tye-dyed T-shirts supplied by the Grateful Dead.

BELOW RIGHT: K2's "American Beauty" design for skis and snowboards, part of a line inspired and authorized by the Grateful Dead.

LEFT: A trimmer Jerry Garcia at his first appearance following his illness in summer 1992, with the Jerry Garcia Band at the Oakland-Alameda County Coliseum, October 30, 1992.

Band, even playing the night that riots associated with the Rodney King police brutality case broke out in downtown San Francisco among other places. In the beginning of May, Garcia was back at the Warfield for more shows with David Grisman, and was reported to be planning a second duo album.

The Dead launched their summer tour for 1992 at Cal Expo on May 18 with a remarkable closer: A medley of the Who's "Baba O'Reilly" and the Beatles' "Tomorrow Never Knows." The tour continued on for more than a month, traveling from Shoreline to Las Vegas; Buffalo, New York; Ohio; Albany, New York; Charlotte, North Carolina; Giants Stadium in New Jersey; RFK Stadium in Washington, D.C.; Pittsburgh; Chicago; and Indiana before concluding back in Ohio on July 1. Perhaps the most notable dates on the tour were the RFK show on June 20, when Bruce Hornsby, who had become a sometime player with the Dead, turned up, and they played "Casey Jones" for the first time since 1984 (Bob Bralove had taken to adding a train sound into the "Drums" section of some shows) and the June 25 show at Soldier Field in Chicago, at which both harmonica great James Cotton and guitarist Steve Miller played.

As they took their summer break, the Dead had a confirmed fall tour that looked as busy as usual. It was set to start August 22 in Veneta, Oregon, include a few Shoreline dates, then head east

and be capped by six nights at Madison Square Garden and six more at Boston Garden, ending on October 1.

Meanwhile, in July, Jerry Garcia and Stonehenge, Ltd. introduced J. Garcia Neckwear, a line of silk neckties. Eight different designs by Garcia, described by the *New York Times* as ranging "from vibrant abstract patterns to a more subdued . . . print of orange fish swimming on a navy sea," went on sale at Bloomingdale's and other department stores for $28.50.

Unfortunately, the next news about Jerry Garcia wasn't so amusing. During the week of August 10, following his 50th birthday, news began to leak out that Garcia was ill again, and Dead Heads feared the worst as the Oregon shows were cancelled. Finally, the band issued a statement: "As the week has passed, we've learned that Jerry Garcia's recuperation will take longer than we'd initially hoped. We remain certain that he will return to full good health, but the rest and care he needs will require us to cancel the fall East Coast tour. Jerry is in the care of a physician at home and is on the mend, but it will take time."

The release quoted Garcia's physician to the effect that the guitarist was suffering from chronic health problems due to smoking, and that Garcia had agreed to a program of stopping smoking, losing weight, exercise, and dietary changes. "We expect to be performing with Jerry before the end of the year," the release noted.

The same expectation seemed to be holding September 22, when Bob Weir turned up at the swanky Tavern on the Green Restaurant in New York to introduce a new line of K2 skis based on the *Panther Dream* book. As usual, part of the proceeds were to go to the Rainforest Action Network and Cultural Survival.

"I think it's basically gonna be nothing but good for us," Weir

LEFT: Bob Weir, who branched out into writing with the children's book *Panther Dream*, published in 1992.

ABOVE: Bill Kreutzmann and Mickey Hart just keep on drumming.

ABOVE RIGHT: Jerry Garcia, who turned artist with his J. Garcia Neckwear in 1992.

RIGHT: Vince Welnick onstage at the Oakland-Alameda County Coliseum, February 1992, where he introduced his first song with the Grateful Dead, "Way to Go Home."

FAR RIGHT: Phil Lesh denied rumors that he intended to retire from the Grateful Dead in the 1990s.

told MTV about Garcia's illness. "Jerry's fine. Jerry's in better shape than I've seen him in years and years. I don't think you're gonna recognize him the next time you see him." Weir said the band would spend November rehearsing and would start playing again in December. This prediction proved true when, on December 2 at McNichols Sports Arena in Denver, the Dead returned to the road. There would be no New Year's shows for 1992, but a 1993 spring East Coast tour was already set, and a full schedule would follow.

As the Grateful Dead approached their 30th year, their legacy, as expressed not only on their records, but also in their 2000+ shows over the years (most of them on tape somewhere) was secure. If they never played another note, they would still be one of the musical phenomena of the twentieth century. As it turned out, the band as we know it would only make it to its 30th year.

Epilogue: 1993-95

The Dead returned to a full schedule of 78 shows in 1993, up from the 57 they played in their abbreviated schedule in 1992 and even more than the 74 they played in 1991. As in 1991, they were ranked the No. 1 concert attraction of the year by *Performance* magazine, grossing more than $44 million.

In October, Jerry Garcia and David Grisman released their second collaboration on Grisman's Acoustic Disc label, a children's recording called *Not For Kids Only*. And on November 1, Grateful Dead Records released (to mail order only) the first in a new series of archival releases, *Dick's Picks, Volume 1*. "Dick" was Dead tape archivist Dick Latvala, and his first pick was a Tampa, Florida, show from December 19, 1973. Unlike the *From the Vault* series, on which the Dead had lavished extensive tape restoration efforts, the *Picks* series was intended to present "as is" recordings, complete with sound imperfections.

On January 19, 1994, the Grateful Dead were inducted into the Rock & Roll Hall of Fame. Jerry Garcia did not attend the ceremony, but the band brought a lifesize cardboard cutout of him to stand in his place.

Garcia did re-surface less than a month later, however, when he married Deborah Koons, a filmmaker, at Christ Episcopal Church in Sausalito.

The year 1994 proceeded much as 1993; still no new album, still plenty of live Dead. The band played 75 shows (accompanied on some by Sting) and grossed a new high of more than $48 million. The only Grateful Dead-related album of 1994 was John Oswald's *Greyfolded*, which took performances of "Dark Star" made between 1968 and 1993 and "processed" them into a single, hour-long work using Oswald's "plunderphonic" techniques: an album to file next to *Infrared Roses*.

1995, the year that marked the Dead's 30th anniversary, at first seemed like just another year in the band's career. The Dead did break tradition by opening the concert year with three shows, February 19-21, at the Delta Center in Salt Lake City. But then it was back to the traditional season opener, the three "Mardi Gras" shows at the Oakland Coliseum Arena, February 24-26. The Spring Tour opened on March 17 with the first of three performances at the Spectrum in Philadelphia, then moved south for three nights at the Coliseum in Charlotte, North Carolina, March 22-24, followed by shows in Atlanta, Memphis, Birmingham, and Tampa.

BELOW LEFT: The Dead in Oakland, May 1993.

ABOVE: Garcia with the Dead at Shoreline, June 4, 1995.

The Dead moved on to the west in May and early June, playing in Las Vegas, Seattle, Portland, and then back to the Shoreline Amphitheater in Mountain View, California. Returning to the East Coast later in the month, they performed a giant show before 100,000 fans in Vermont, then did stadium dates with Bob Dylan in Washington, D.C., East Rutherford, N.J., and Chicago, where the summer tour ended on July 9 at Soldier Field.

But the tour was not without incident. At Robert F. Kennedy Memorial Stadium in Washington, D.C., a fan was struck by lightning. More seriously, on July 2, in Noblesville, Indiana, a group of ticketless fans attempted to break into a show at the Deer Creek Amphitheatre, tearing down a fence and attacking police.

For the first time in their career, the Dead were forced to cancel the next night's show. Then, on July 5, at a campground near the Riverport Amphitheatre outside St. Louis, where the band was appearing, a deck collapsed on 100 fans seeking refuge from a rainstorm. Dozens were injured, some critically.

With the Summer Tour completed, the band was on hiatus until September 13, when the Fall Tour was set to start at Boston Gardens. The tour called for the Dead to play six nights in Boston, then six at Madison Square Garden in New York City, starting on September 21, with further dates in Philadelphia and Toronto and an eventual end-of-tour show on October 22 in San Francisco. (And the album on which the Dead had been working was set for release on October 3.)

On July 17, Jerry Garcia checked into the Betty Ford Center in Rancho Mirage, California, complaining of an addiction to heroin. Garcia stayed at the clinic for two weeks, but then went home, apparently to celebrate his 53rd birthday on August 1. During the first week in August, however, friends persuaded him to try treatment again, and Garcia checked in to Serenity Knolls, a drug and alcohol treatment center north of San Francisco.

Around 4 a.m. on August 9, during a routine bed-check, a counselor discovered Garcia in his room comatose and without a pulse. Attempts to revive him were unsuccessful, and he was pronounced dead at 4:23 a.m. The Marin County coroner's office reported that Garcia appeared to have died of natural causes, and an autopsy was performed.

The response to Garcia's death by Dead Heads was overwhelming. Impromptu wakes were held in the Haight-Ashbury in San Francisco, at Strawberry Fields in Central Park, New York City, at the Lincoln Memorial in Washington, D.C., in Griffith Park in Los Angeles, and on Independence Mall in Philadelphia, among other places.

"There's no way to measure his greatness or magnitude," said Bob Dylan. "I don't think any eulogizing will do him justice." Yet there were further eulogies from a variety of musicians, including Willie Nelson, Carlos Santana, Sammy Hagar, and Smokey Robinson. In San Francisco, Mayor Frank Jordan ordered flags lowered to half-staff and flew a tie-dyed flag from City Hall.

Bob Weir was on tour with Rob Wasserman and the backup band they now called Ratdog, scheduled to play a show on the evening of August 9 at the Hampton Beach Casino Ballroom in Hampton, New Hampshire. Weir went on with the show, telling the crowd, "Our departed friend, if he proved anything to us, proved music could make sad times better." He closed the show with "Knockin' On Heaven's Door." The next day, Weir cancelled his tour and returned to San Francisco.

ABOVE: On August 13, a memorial was held for Garcia in Golden Gate Park.

Jerry Garcia's funeral was held at St. Stephen's Episcopal Church in Belvedere, California, on Friday, August 11. 250 mourners, including members of Garcia's family and of the Grateful Dead, and such guests as Bob Dylan, Ken Kesey, Bruce Hornsby, and Bill Walton, attended. The eulogy was given by lyricist Robert Hunter. Two days later, Hunter and members of the Dead also remembered Garcia at a memorial at Golden Gate Park in San Francisco attended by 25,000.

But earlier in 1995, Jerry Garcia provided his own epitaph and a statement about the Grateful Dead journey itself when he was interviewed for a cable TV series called "The Movie That Changed My Life." Garcia chose *Abbott and Costello Meet Frankenstein*, the 1948 comedy-thriller, recalling that he had first seen it with his mother when he was seven; it was then he had first heard what he later termed "the call of the weird."

"I have a general fascination with the bizarre that comes directly from that movie," he said. "I don't think I knew that before I saw that movie, that there are things that are really weird and there are people who are concerned with them." Garcia laughed, and continued, "That became important to me, and I guess I thought to myself on some level, 'I think I want to be concerned with things that are weird.' I think that seems interesting to me because it seems like fun. And that is in fact who I am."

Index

Page numbers in *italics* refer to illustrations

Acknowledgments
Special thanks to Ed Perlstein; Herb Greene; and Martin Leffer of Not Fade Away Graphics for their help with this project. Thanks also go to Jean Chiaramonte Martin, the editor; Adrian Hodgkins, the designer; and Elizabeth A. McCarthy, the indexer.

Picture Credits
Brompton Photo Library: 9(both).
Chris Fallo: 4, 10(left), 62(top), 68(top), 69(both).
Greg Gaar: 33(bottom), 61.
Claude Gassian: 28(both), 30-31, 31.
Globe Photos: 6-7, 22.
Herb Greene: 8, 12-13, 14, 15(all 3), 16, 17, 18, 19, 23, 25(bottom), 48(both), 49, 66(top), 72, 73.
Lisa Law: 20
Martin Leffer: 75(bottom).
Jim Marshall: 20-21, 21, 25(top), 26-27, 37(bottom).
Bob Minkin: 44-45, 56-57, 64, 65(bottom), 66(bottom), 70, 71(top), 72-73, 74, 77(bottom left).
Ed Perlstein; 1, 33(top), 34, 34-35, 38(both), 40, 40-41, 42-43, 44, 52(top), 54-55, 55, 62(bottom), 71(bottom).
Bruce Polonsky: 5, 10-11, 29, 32(both), 36-37, 36, 37(top), 50(both), 50-51, 52(bottom), 53, 58-59, 60(both), 63(bottom), 65(top), 79.
Retna: Jay Blakesberg 10(right), 11(left), 67, 68(bottom), 76(left), 77(top and bottom right), 78-79(all 3); Adrian Boot 39; Larry Busacca 11(right); Larry Hulst 46-47, 76(right); Paul Lemaszewsky 63(top).
UPI/Bettmann Newsphotos: 24-25, 75(top).
Tie-dyes by Not Fade Away Graphics, Inc.